I0742098

Our
Love's
Creation

Our Love's Creation

By Anthony Smith

Shoestring Book Publishing, Maine, USA

Our Love's Creation

Paperback

ISBN: 978-1-943974-12-2

Library of Congress Preassigned Control Number: 2017957626

Published by;
Shoestring Book Publishing
Maine, USA

Layout and design by Shoestring Book Publishing
Publishers since 2012

For information address;
Shoestring Book Publishing c/o Allan Emery
495 Penobscot Avenue
Millinocket Maine 04462

shoestringpublishing4u@gmail.com
www.shoestringbookpublishing.com

Dedicated to my Dear sweet wife, Maureen

Distinct change came about me for the good, when we met. Late November, 1986, the then, Miss Maureen, Fiona Dunkley came into my life, her Anglo-Indian loveliness existed then as it does today, and it has never changed. With those beautiful brown eyes, an angelic soul, making another soul happy. Although we did have things on our minds back then. Myself from personal trauma, trying to cope, and you Maureen, your thoughts for your dear sweet mother, Mrs. Patricia Dunkley, who was back home in Mussoorie in the Northern State of Uttar Pradesh, India, with your mind swayed.

Circumstances beyond our control preventing our union, it was without hindrance we got along like friends. I was very much in love with you but, it was neither here nor there. Difficult for both of us, since I was healing slowly. Maureen, your trips back and forth to India were mighty epic, with distance alone. We would be together for a few weeks, then for two years almost, at a time, we'd suffer separately.

'Our Love's Creation' was shaped first by your mother, who bore you, then, succeeded to bring out this devotion you have, your Catholic Faith has never faltered. Your worship in private is so closely connected to God, that I feel Him when I'm with you. I really do wish your mum, and my dad had been alive to give their blessings at our wedding. They were most certainly in our hearts that day, and like every day, they are always in our prayers.

Making friends is your passion. It was when you met Charlotte White, an Anglo herself, who got us to meet her family. Her husband, Errol, and two daughters, Natalie and Hayley. In your absence they took it upon themselves to make me a part of their family, and I hadn't felt this close, even to my own, I really wasn't coping very well without you, Therefore, Charlotte, Errol, and you two girls, I sincerely thank you from the bottom of my heart.

Anthony Smith

Maureen

A classic love story .....

Table Of Contents

Foreword

Titus is alive. For us who are familiar with the English language, we are pleased to hand you this book as proof of the unbroken continuum of his contribution to the teas, jams & biscuits of poetic differentiation.

Shakespeare, Milton, Bronte, Kipling, Dickens, Eliot and now Llewellyn. To read these words by Titus once, we are doubly rewarded with second or third readings of his words as multiple sips of his tea of semantics and wonderful nibbles on the biscuits of his meanings offer us sublime looks into the human experience.

Titus is the ultimate writer, the deep conscious use of codex explains in English, as it matures. It is well worth your time uncovering the true depth of his serious works. By the way, his love poetry speaks for itself.

Michael Thomas

My Friend & Mentor, Andre

Our eminent guest, a poet who has given me the greatest pleasure of words indiscriminately, to have us feast our eyes on what can only be described a banquet. Exuberant praise indeed, to say Andre, I have never met such a modest man, such as yourself.

I have upheld the synonym used for books other than this that Andre speaks with the utmost respect of, 'Sir' to me. It is his wish not mine, a man who has enriched me with a kind humble grace, a pride of place I find myself in, to learn.

…, and so, I give you, Andre Emmanuel Bendavi ben-YEHU

◆ ◆ ◆

Greetings to One and to All that these letters may read.

To talk about Sir Titus Llewellyn, and his literary works, or of his life, is not an easy task, for one to have to count and select words that show their magnetic force.

The poetic works by Sir Titus are true lines of artistry, knowledge and emotional experiences that inspire and edify the readers' intellectuality and spiritual growth.

Sir Titus is a Poet, Master of the Quill — that I consider a protégé of Minerva and Venus; — and an Ambassador of Apollo, for he is also a man of science and philosophy.

The interpretation of love — in the sense of the union of two souls and body's fusion of energy — comes from the Sanskrit root, and togetherness and compassion; friendship and charity comes from the Greek root. So, a perfect union would be the one that has the two meanings in one purpose.

When romance is the subject, Sir Titus knows how to present "Oyster's with their flawless pearls, the words from the art's ocean" of life. I am positive to say that those who read this romantic book by Sir Titus will enjoy a literary ambrosia.

Wisdom, Peace and Love.

October 30, 2017

Andre Emmanuel Bendavi ben-YEHU

Preface

Dear Maureen,

Late November 1986, when you, Miss Maureen Dunkley, stepped into my life. It was for me 'love at first sight.' Both of us had plenty going on, I respected the little time we had together most certainly. It reveres you in some way as, 'the elusive woman', and this you are, as it shall always will be.

Very much in love, unable to express in words like I do now I tried, but my poetry was completely dire to publish a book one day it was not a good idea. Unless the rusty skills I have in English language were improved. Then when those needs are met, it should be in depth, every part of you.

It is hoped it will stir some excitement for the readers, like how I felt, when out of the blue a written airmail envelope landed through my letter box. Written by you among other things, confirming for sure, your love for me. Oh, how I waited for that moment. It answered my dreams. That letter along with others is locked away now with other keepsakes.

Now, I know poetry isn't your thing, but I know my efforts and hopefully some memorable lines will highlight the past, my intended in-being, namely you. The simple things in life please us both as well, our similar upbringings, as we've regularly mentioned about our ways. For me, your Faith so very private and with your perseverance towards God, you do so without harbouring any prejudice whatsoever. Contentment, the simple things in life do please, and never too much is said about trivial things. The God given grace to observe your loveliness as nature itself intended, you have become the sweetest and most endearing, gentle soul.

Your bountiful heart pleases me no end, as you seem to keep many people in high spirits as well. This gift your mother gave to you, is envied. It is my best intention to do likewise with words. Worthy attempt is made to lift all hearts with 'Our Love's Creation.' –

Your Dearest Husband,

Tony

ACKNOWLEDGEMENTS

Had it not been for you, I'd not have found my love
RAY SMITH, [brother]

Advice on this lengthy wait of ours,
giving the idea of writing those memoirs
SHEILA NASIR

Being on hand in a social sense,
during, and after Maureen's return
SUE CRANG, ALICIA CARRUTHERS, LIZ MALFOY

Making me a part of your endearing family,
taking in all I had to say, and listening
contently, without any exasperations.
**THE WHITE FAMILY
CHARLOTTE, ERROL, NATALIE AND HAYLEY**

For putting our welfare first, with your beautiful heart
DR. RABIA DABO

Our closest friends nearby who are always there
**PAM & JOHN McCUAIG, SYLVIE FELLS, LYNNETTE &
NIGEL FOAD, GLORIA HATTON-TATE, JOHN WOOD,
DAVE GURUNG, DARRYL ANDERSON**

Poets and friends who are more like family now
**NATASHA & KINZA MUBASHER, JOSEPHINE VELLA,
DEBBIE ALTIPARMAKIS, DENNIS WHITE, J TODD
UNDERHILL, JUDY CAROLYN ROBERTS, MOTHI
CHANDAR**

Our friend in London, who is a very dear lady
DR. MAI YAMANI

Introduction To Praxiteles

Our Love's Creation

Genesis 1:27 - 'God created man in His own image, in the image of God He created him'

The title of this book came about by that Genesis quote. The rubber stamp so to speak of man's image and what is pertained from it, magnifies beyond belief. 'Our Love's Creation'. holding this image for Praxiteles, [a sculptor], considering the fact that his works were quite magnificent.

From his hands to mine, I summon the poem, *'LOVE PERFECTING PRAXITELES'*, and it is so unlike my other poems

Xenofontus who was commissioner of works then, in Kos, 330 BC, the wishes of its people was to have a reputable work of art, and Aphrodite presented to the town. Praxiteles was asked to do the job, [and Pliny speaks of two creations.] One in reverence the other more revealing. The public were bemused by what they had seen, obviously the version they were presented with was not to their liking. There was no problem installing their wish.
As for falling in love with one's own creation, it can be admired from a distance to believe I had in fact. Praxiteles gave worthy explanation to Xenofontus, which had him nodding his approval.

From, *'Love Perfecting, Praxiteles'*
'I cannot speak for others, how the almighty it speaks of duty, only faith will know, beauty, love appears to what Aphrodite has, the world still in waiting shows, is a love worth creating.'

Love Perfecting, Praxiteles - Sestina

Dedicated to my wife, Maureen, who has shaped
me as a man, and thus shaping love as a whole.

Medallion representing Praxiteles

The unlikely story of the sculptor, **Praxiteles**, who falls in love
with a marble creation, of his own making, 'Aphrodite'
Enter: Praxiteles, Xenofontos,
Location: Island of Kos, Gaiou Stertinou Xenofontus,
Chief of construction

Prelude

i

Praxiteles, love for this island Kos, is warmth in waiting
Its people have forbidden love from parading all beauty,
Drawn from stone, may it be indulgence pray, your duty?
To overlay the nether regions fully without cloth creating
Coy, enact with inhibition to deny that man the almighty
God, show a dispassionate womanly shape as Aphrodite.

Praxiteles gazes at the block of marble
ii
Is this beginning of a lasting relationship with Aphrodite?

To be conscripted her freedom swore virtue, 'I am waiting'
Still, for some of your time for mine includes an almighty
God, who is blind in actual fact, also to show us His beauty
To cast his naked shadow over Kos, It would be the duty
Of lasting freedom, to find the feel for touch it is creating.

iii

Over whether safe or not storm were brewing, my creating
With this myth, I'll show mere leniency, towards Aphrodite
Humble gratitude to hide what all gods do, a sense of duty
Impounded by worshipping woman a wise detect, awaiting
Weakly, a position I'd rather not say sneakily, like if beauty
Were it to allow me a full façade, worship what is almighty.

iv

Typically the rear, rough outlook of pity it came, almighty
And from its privileged parts, are kept mindful if creating
Nothing more than what cannot hide, my love for beauty.
Believe me, I, soothing this delicate matter over Aphrodite,
To chip away the part of one's creation love I find waiting
Often you will find, it shapes the man with a sense of duty.

v.

Behind a mere back chat to think of ordinary women duty,
To explore, as women pass, the improbable once almighty
Trait is offered, disdain does harm an offensive, in waiting
Forbidden pity it would eschew, replying to when creating
Blind a town the myth then, it is more the pity, Aphrodite
To feel this power overcome me shown as apparent beauty.

Aphrodite is revealed, it shocks the people of Kos
Xenofontus:

vi

This stolen sanctuary you've admitted treason isn't beauty
Yet from Knidos where covenant is prime, my weary duty
To reveal the utmost chaos going on, it dignifies Aphrodite,

4   Anthony Smith

'Rising from foam', if the compound, shines an almighty - **Prax.**
Spirit it is renown as far from disbelieving, we are creating
Havoc, to digress as far as Venus, then I will go on waiting.

vii

I cannot speak for others, how the almighty it speaks of duty,
only faith will know, beauty, love appears to what Aphrodite
has, the world still in waiting shows, is a love worth creating.

Love & Marriage

Marriage, and our time together has given
Replicas of paradise, believed to be heaven
On earth, - here, love in the highest brings
To mind, feelings are when the heart sings.

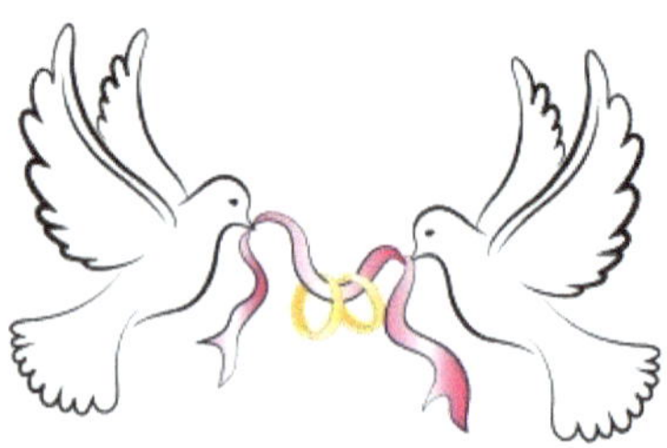

Dancing Forever – Acrostic

Descending are the angels of romance
Abstaining thrift on greeting man's desire
Now showing somewhat freely to the dance,
Contained since space between the two require,
Insightful an allegiance loved much higher,
Naively as the true soul marital,
Gives tenderly to guidance they befall.

Footsteps which forever shall begin,
Oratory movements through the curve,
Returning true like lovers here within,
Evolving out he speaks and she reserve,
Viable that dance has to akin,
Each holding on to life, a death preserve
Remains from any wonder why we spin.

Daydreams

Perhaps your virtue makes a perfect peace,
attain from far your lease its motion yearns
subservient, whilst natures woo plays turns,
supplies the sun, and yet by grace release
insatiable desire, it leaves life's form.
Ornate, whose love between suppliant lie
nemoral shows the study of conform -
by what appears it seems there's you and I
unknown to woodland stow so paths may cross
renditions walk ways; start where firm reply,
now means who'd keep in thought is who it was;
said something of their lover, as to why?

Love Letters

The enigmatic flow of inks survive
Upon the paper dried and this we see,
As verse which brings a character alive
Which gives a true account of guarantee.

WE bind the words together for all else
Deceives to leading mistresses astray,
Can in effect deliver them in quells
Whilst having time correcting an affray.

You'll notice how varieties have grades,
To elevate the smooth appearance for
A fountain pen to serenade fair trades
And having faith in women he'll adore.

A style that is as lucrative advance,
To notice that the ink is running dry
Leaving them a line in true romance,
Another one to make the ladies cry.

He, Finding Us Both

Born from a whim that one November night,
Accounts, as true fate that a moment be right.
To consider the trust of belonging were there,
If misguided or found as a warmth of fine air.
My first sight of food led was appetite heaped,
By awareness the sight of her beauty I peep'd
Amongst others I coped to be near if indeed,
Was the best of ten minutes, sufficient a need.

To imagine my luck was perfected than dreamt
By her gaze as a torment the sweet after scent,
Would on offer give love, an affection to bliss,
She occasioned on leaving a chance not to miss.
I encouraged her pause to be given one chance
Of a life time to forage the next night in trance.

And on meeting the next was a night to recall,
To remember the sight of her soft bleary eyed
The occasion had grown from so little but all,
I have eyes for adds while so elusive a guide.
I found sympathy waiting a past had matured,
By desire and a life time, an angel who hides,
Be it fate was to find to be God's to be lured
From this heavenly glory the love He divides.

She is born of the Faith and is closest to Him,
I am wanton of hope that true love will reside
In a wonderful moment this love from a whim
I can vouch we'll together be joined in abide.
In the time of passing, love the collected oath,
Guarantees this loyalty of His, finding us both.

Prolong to the Chase – Sestina

Ephemeroptera
O' to enchant thee where naiad or the colloquial nymph,
Hovers affection, showing signs have bared hardened wings
To appreciate that May devotion considers it as ' kiss chase',
For it pardons all emotion, were it to rendezvous by chance,
Believing an early summer shows how to cherish both, as if,
The sun leapt out, between the stages of two giant strides!

That spring and summer promised zeal with longing strides,
The shortest love on record to adore than outwit this nymph,
For the sake of romance can one's treasure beloved be, as if?
Each an angel, where tender love prenuptial spread of wings,
Escapes for affection as the darling buds of May gives chance,
They too would settle down to the discovery of a godly chase.

Whilst dormant lie of being submerged in an unlike chase,
The feeding on the diatom would embrace residing strides,
Preparing years for pride digests like, as if we had no chance!
Like nothing, as if nothing else much dared to find a nymph,
Existing like treasure, like life itself discovers no more wings,
Sweeping promiscuity aside this sole role uniting of what if…?

….If luck were to depend on the outcome, a meeting with if,
To communicate with, on this occasion, helpless in that chase,
Having disaster to deal with a premature all, - but for our wings,
Oblige the dreams where our be known to all has left strides,
Leading where there is to adore all the emotions of the nymph,
If selected were to fond relate an appeal to it upon that chance!

Would leave in rapture the beloved kiss for the sake of chance,
To rendezvous with, has challenged ill waits for we cannot if,
We remember the day as long, than the aftermath sweet nymph,
For whose instinct to cherish affection to, we devote one chase,
Torments the runaway friend fleeing from that which if strides,

Were after all replies of such dormant signs not those with wings.

When briefly we are to fear the darling embrace of godly wings,
Attached, and forever it seems to have caught us up, by chance,
That we are just able to felicitate moments where angel strides,
Having the new day indicate to us that everyday be joyful, as if,
Dying didn't matter, that the spark of any passion has its chase,
And fond relations will have to adore you, the sweetest nymph!

Ask to question the wings of nature should explore befitting if,
Where chance to falter still relies on fate, of prolonging chase,
Times I've turned, making strides on who what I'd call a nymph.

Love's Impromptu - Prelude

I do accept that the cold of nature in my heart,
Has encouraged a wide preconception, hatred.
Wholeheartedly mine, for which blame in part,
Some discomfort shown, to have been invaded.
Dense as a means to portray what is neglected,
You'll have sunlight every day, not to discover
The meaning of life, had you noticed, detected
That my darkness under cover, shows no other.

I'm determined though to find what of sunlight,
And for any other there is this smooth lack-lustre -
Passionate glimpse, something more than slight,
Opening any wonder as to why I cannot muster.

To penetrate as light, by what it feels to gather,
That things are wholly now, to contend myself,
If not, to forget love around me, a world rather,
Forgotten, it has to impose upon merely wealth?
Others seem unabashed where there is mention
Of money, another ill trait, for which this peril
Evolves around, it seems there is with intention
Rising above the other, a hint of whose is feral.

A love, I can no doubt understand if being close
Without you, to attach whereby it were necessary
To match for detail spreading, love which grows,
Dissection of a nature not as sad but just as wary.

I continue in the hope of lost abandonment, shy.
Why that is, existence is important to the likes;
There are moments when unlike dark, I can try -
With much determined effort, sun-light strikes.

Besides What's Beautiful

Imposed upon how beautiful they are,
the eyes have found deception with a wink,
a smile would hold to ransom what to think,
with whom for looking at it was not far
the situations when you speak as well,
how fancy full with intrigue does one feel,
to steal the looks off one, a smile to sell,

And from who spoke was telling her they're real.
I hasten not to gaze than stray for keeps,
offending that to write about them shows
alliance with the eyes of one who peeps,
shall not disclose so near than he who knows.
And yet such modesty would persevere,
it seems a wish more dreamy than sincere.

An Auspicious Bond

Love's incredible dream leaves us languishing among the stars
the moonlight, buoyancy enough to hang what is love's light,
whereby journeys we sought together leaves suddenly for Mars,
what seems to drift, it seems we're caught by nothing, right?

Then let's for once, not disturb the sky closing in on our night
twinkling an embellish, like stars outreach their eyes like ours
would transcribe looking into, writing the Psalms clearly bright
bringing peace, the silence writes with ease what love empowers.

Parting Through a Wood

Titania, of her mission with her sprites, on
the trail of Whether or Not.

From this fine wood stow greenery didst find?
Hast merriment the charms the blue bells sound
Amidst the frolics, tulips, daffodils,
And seedlings, they'd be signs of nurture fills,
Suffice like spore and saunter fleece, the ground!
From thence a smitten breeze thereafter stirred,
Where mischievous of trees surround indent,
And fairies, who'd I'd never thought were meant,
Were there, yet unaware of tales that has occurred!

Undergrowth, to be the lore of the forgotten 'we',
Magical, tho' having been mindful, art what shrubbery
You've parted to find such tales thereafter -
Squeaks of laughter makes; the squirrels tell thee...
Something is lurking-
Some maternal instinct, woo working -
Some kind endeared to stalking,
Some fearful tale you'd seek not want for talking!

Before time is this - - from whose it seeks forever,
Never meant to be found before, then the believers
Of who through tall sward it finds, are trail weavers,
Giving to children, this dream for turn or whether.

How Far, How Bright a Love

What shone so bight the night a thousand stars,
Gave shrug to, love becomes fate's pulling part
Soothing distance, I discount the many scars,
As many thoughts conceal, my bleeding heart.
Rewriting dreams that wide awake can't steal,
Would find from deep within, the utmost care.

To think how lowly ebbs have pushed I kneel,
And pray for once, a dream it might find there.
Why breathing in so deep, love would escape,
Entranced by faith, your giving me would sell
Incensed by what appeared a conscience gape,
The first the last I've read; your voice did tell.
It came from faith's most certain, future bright
Perhaps I'd think for once, it's proved so right.

Collective Thoughts

Love has created an endearing way;
of collecting thoughts.
The years we've carried, are put away,
my mind though, concedes to distance
between our pulling love towards
to stretch further, any imagination,
longing, it becomes the broken heart,
it should, no further more.
Loss has overwhelmed me from stealing,
the dreams I still imbibe on nightly.
Though briefly together, we are…
I would cherish this togetherness again,
If only once, now scarred, it is for always,
by what can ill affect the said illusion -
By my adding length to our time apart,
it creates this opus, upon all whereabouts,
belonging to is to reach each other,
it's heavenly as anyone could imagine.
To encourage my heart from not aching
lost cause has discovered overbearing pain,
of which the clouds hold in passing,
tiny reliefs of sunshine peeping through.
It develops myth into this very subject
in conclusion to trap all sunlight keenly
I am to advance alas, a self-impasse,
prolonging to keep us, our souls retained
sincerely as my heart is to encourage
wise reasoning why God had not intervened.
If there's godly else description, to impart,
upon writing you into this myth.
An elusive who inscribes all this whereabouts,
it is to incorporate what these virtues are
Heavenly abide are collective thoughts.

The Day I Met an Angel

God seemed to appear, when at my lowest
Took upon Himself or when she'd stir,
He'd then confide an angel who thou knowest,
Brought me from the edge, the dark demur,
Then came the words, tibi magno cum amor.

Common Courtesy to a Passing Glance

She's touched by the enamour of my ways
And slightly as her head so turns would choose,
Towards me, that she'd turn again, it says;
She's touched.

A gentleness which if indeed 'twould use,
To smile back, would encourage her displays,
I'd tilt my head with no need to refuse.

I too would have loved to use a paraphrase,
In which to dance around her, such are views!
Belonged to face, oh my, and also praise!
She's touched.

On First Approach – Semi-tetra

Amor Primus

Breathe a sigh of passion, a task,
too beautiful for love to ask,
How coy, they mask?

Two lovers, whom upon each wait
In hover, show their love as bait
anticipate....

Let's instil a comfort to thirst,
our situation, first things first
we're both best nursed.

Willingness to approach with
her, often laughter, to at least stir...
one another.

Breathless, a Sigh

First the sigh, a love first met;
The time it took for the next,
As breathless greets each sigh repeats.
Again, life or death it were.

Life is such had not we met,
I may have before then, wept
But crying without, not to doubt
Loving were waiting for me.

First the sigh a love first met;
Before my eyes, the sky she lit
Stood, before why, lifting me high,
Above, a sigh where love roams.

Soul to Soul

If beauty were reflected purely bliss,
the touchless work of art to all who stood,
above us like they would not render this
admired from far but left alone for good.

How sad it would be now to read a book,
about long distance love and needless woe
to escalate the grief between them grow
and with that absence need I take a look?

I ask you had the surface tension broke,
the water on my face would be the same
as if my loneliness were such to blame,
that need be seen too shy before I woke.

The settled waters here are not disturbed;
the peaceful soul is resting unperturbed.
Bespoke would shiver ripples by the wake,
an agitated soul should not exist,
but anything that utters from the lake,
suspecting if panic should still persist.

I ask you for the sake of nature's force,
regard the breeze for all the voices made,
to welcome you alive and I of course,
am dead, until such time reflections fade.

A ripple is like walking from a dream,
a swivel of contentment without thought,
for who you are and who it is you seem,
will bring the calm again and not distraught.
A soul from true perspective keeps veneer,
from anything that seems to be this near.

Home from Home

With this invite, could her smile be richly given,
to dwell upon the warmth from it maintained?
So be, who may have burdened you their living,
for once it feels like home our hopes contained.

The Furthest Love

Love beyond the illusion is the deepest love I know as it never quite

hurts you like true love does and that is why I love you from afar.

How Close to Dreams We Are

How subtle we have nurtured love our own,
Romance would open portals to those dreams,
Where neither can more love be trod alone
Together in this midst of those it seems.

Would cherish you as part of me that weeps,
Auspicious that the inner depths to peace
Shall stay awake my love, so love it keeps
The pleasure from the hug my golden fleece.

Our hands are clasped in raptures of delight
Which forage first like comfort from just one
Who pleasures us the most during the night
If dreams indeed come true, a quest be won.

I cannot vouch how close to dreams we are,
Just hold on tight there cannot be too far.

Oncidium – An Orchid

Oncidium, referred to as the dancing lady of delight
Relevant clusters have infused a cocoa bean, a slight
Chocolate flavour, a sensitive taste, the hours seed,
How fragrance profuse to quote, her mellow plead
Impassioned by surreal, stands best inside, a garden
Dreams adorn her praise to spare, a winter's harden.
Majestic perhaps, to conceal the orchid, any mishaps.

Love Portrayed, Cinquain Form Chain

Epics,
weave lyrical
composing, devoting, portraying,
maidenhead fern, love's lantern,
verdant.

Prelude
to culminate
unfolding, beginning, following,
prominence, a shroud floral,
landscape.

Coupled,
with highlights
proposing, displaying, exposing
visuals, you can't explain,
rephrase.

Antinuptial

Woman, love creates what is a colliquable essence
Your elegance is corporeal to conceal essential oils,
Romantic remedy, this scapegrace trait quiescence,
Love's surquedry belonging to my love, it so spoils

Merely, to bring from worship, often, I overly praise,
Being ante-nuptial, an event to serve you kowtow,
Succeeds to broaden calm, beyond sepentrion sprays,
Gifting youth, a mountain's trust, and strength avow.

Your spirit, to be drenched, by love, and true feeling,
Of warmth, the mackinaw has restored in me to give,
The blessing of 'adamantine', has promised healing -
Permit we step into wild romance, this love we live.

On Fragile Wings, Orseis

Orseis, where both of us in passing,
None would have suspected from her kind,
Fragmentations who, from goodness passing
Rightly had we stopped to speak our mind
And not to have forgot that what we'd find
Gives such a lot of joy by such discrete.

It's admirably an etiquette of care,
Let's not so over dramatise the greet,
Each has but let one know when nice is there.
Whereas 'twas blindly dealt that why instead,
It is the words you write, the kind of peace
Not knowing who you are, but what you said,
Gift wise said few reminders on release
Sophisticating ways she's compromised

On wings there lifts a virtue where the moon,
No weight at all can lift your once immune,
For freedom has been blessed as the reserve,
Remaining of durations of these lifts,
A freedom of the openness which gifts!

Great onus on the impetus hors d'oeuvre
Intention as the best preludes as such,
let wings of nature spree their vast outlay
Entwined with one another's like today!
What is it that the butterfly does next?
Negotiating flowered plants and mates,
Glides amorously close and procreates
Survival tend change one's written text.

Option was, this was not just any one,
Nothing can compare, that with it done,
Found something of the lore a query set
Reviving what it was, when first we met,
As if the human form were normal trace,
Gamin of the sheltered haunt 'tis grace,
Inflicted by the care it carried out;
Let loose among the lost, the most devout

Evolving and escaping a retrieve,
Where luck would have it nobody's reprieve,
Is certain let alone the time, it flies.
How freedom would make affluent surprise,
Getting there and back, in one safe swoop,

Protect the love praised, rather not lets us coop.

Your Modesty

Your modesty is such, a red standard rose

Why, Solitude?

Why solitude has succeeded to be charmed, by nature;
Alone, in ember, quiver not to resent, some bitter twist
Of fate, tempting to devour a phrase or two, a matcher
Who makes well executed remark, oblivion does persist
In detriment to unravel with agony, I may not complain?
As a result, fear extends what might have been encased,
 I am in two minds to think excessively, a find displaced.

I do embark upon loves fury, my bowels prolapse inside
By what had shattered me earlier, truth, it would control,
A vain reproach describing stature, and stride for stride,
Invasion, it will accrue what is an allegoric theme, lyrical,
Denouement dark, a myth associated with consequential
Tempting the storm clouds, to evolve they plead satirical
Shapes, demons portraying menace to equip as bona fide.

Fear Not My Love

The fear that our love was reprimanded,
Has since resolved itself, and yet I fear –
I am given bearing, since the distant self
Correlates to findings, something to keep
For old time's sake, it hangs on to, hope.
'Biannual man', I am called from waiting.

Since time and I have travelled, awaiting
My love to return, what is reprimanded,
Is, the uncaring of other's, while I hope,
I haven't suffered much, I can still fear,
The loss now married, nothing will keep
A life for a life, this reflection of myself.

I cannot get to grips if always by myself,
To fear a past, how close to not waiting,
Have I aspired to move on, what I keep: –
Advice I'm given, my being reprimanded
I don't think thoughts unknown do fear
To survive on trust, it is to raise all hope.

Suspected as a man by many, I can hope
The woman of my dreams holds myself
Esteem, the good grace to seek out fear,
To face those demons fraught in waiting,
Impatiently, I may falter, if reprimanded
By weakness to fail then what do I keep?

To have a clear conscience is one I keep,
And will have until time is frail of hope,
A future world exists, am I reprimanded
To forward notice, and to resign myself,
Obsessional death, this stillness waiting?
Has given the calm perspective over fear.

Time and closure have resulted the fear,
Infinity, as life shall go on, words I keep
Shall forever be in your debt for waiting,
Not once did I feign desire and my hope
Is bound by movement, leading this self,
Contained by true love, it is reprimanded.
It is not too late to keep words of hope,
You have been reprimanded to seek self-
Assured, as was my waiting will not fear.

When First We Met,

A Second Ought in Time

Sincerely is the man whose love conveys
A woman who held first a second glance
Never to be forgotten, when he says…
My love I did but turn, but only once.

A single turn would simply mean to know
What falling for the first time does rely?
I closed my eyes, and saw the next how slow
It took to love again, our first goodbye.

To think of losing after first we met,
The second time of asking myself first,
It was to be the first, the time was set,
To find a way to keep myself immersed.

It masks a simple parting from a rhyme,
Two lines of four, we two are set to time.

So Rare a Flower

Her idle charms, fear for where
Can love find: so far yet near?
Where the incalculable share,
A moment of luck becomes, we're
This close to, once in a life time;
When two become once in awhile,
 It would seem, loves, infinite prime,
Not much is said, than with a smile.
And so we must now let assume,
 For the moment; had neither met,
The chance in wait, an anxious bloom
So rare was there to have love let.

The New Day

Duly I take not for granted,
A rose from its stem without cause;
To keep forever, most enchanted
We share such time without a pause.

Nymphs, Angelic Notes

Almost to the point of recognition
Is that we know the stranger who
Shall show only kindness as the few
Helpers in life who are by definition
Angels, finding them, is so precious
Hopes are one day, one will bless us.

Courtiers who have blessed us each
Exquisite thoughts on praising sings
Nonchalant notes aid gladly, a reach
Inhibit scenes where angels have wings;
Zealous are we who have yet to free
Apparent doubt so let our minds see.

Rectify feeling, to aid you good health
Achieved by believing this fact, your,
Comfort has such kindness, its wealth
Includes a care of attention you adore
Orbed as such aided by this free spirit,
Nature intends to think you'd inherit.

Love in the Highest - Reverse Abecedarian

Zenith! The highest point to which furthest
You can go, what my faith has surely seen;
Xylot you have sweetened with a once keen
Woman of my dreams, love, it has a surface
Viewing her this welcome, love's attribute,
Under this gaze I can but reach for always,
Taking her, without forgetting how so cute
She is, the promise of good things God says
Remember, He does listen, but it is without...
Question, to answer first, with its time delays
Perhaps where love's concerned, little doubt?

Of each occasion, their hearts are hovering,
Nonchalantly where doubt will roam, I feel,
Maybe confidence assured, without bothering
Let us determine the well-meaning man, real...
Kindly theories relate to these actions, close...
Join with a well-intended reason, to compare,
In depth the truth of man by what he shows
Help to understand a women for she to care
Given plenty, how a material wealth is taken,
Fairly, since love has become within, received
Endless words I would consider, will awaken
Defining death and dreams, if it was believed
Caring, as whereabouts she'll go, this she will,
Belong to you forever and avow unending to
Attach herself to love's following, anon until…

Love's Reminisce

Breathe in the first I say, and simply take'
The dreams of love, as ones I duly keep
A wife, who is my sleeping beauty, sleep,
A dawn would have awoken, tho forsake.
She cannot vouch the day will be as long,
A moment to have woken from the past
A dream 'twill last as long, but not as fast
Whose tale continues fabled, lies among,
As many years ago, remain then, young, --

It is the blessed state your stillness bore,
To wake upon the kiss, the moment let,
Begins the first and last, our eyes beset,
A smile, I dare not say, one can't ignore.
Adhere to still remember dreams explore.

A Dream of If

First sighting of she, who's allure incensed
Love thereby judging her, by this denote,
Whilst she the giver this the task against,
My better judgement seen as asymptote.
To feel, accepted, tho her eyes conceal
Light to behold me, self-abandoned, why?
Invite has consigned one's utterance feel,
Without a word, our time, a brief descry.
Thou art care she would gift love's charity
Some soul-worthy gesture once acquired
Giving thine own worth's amount, clarity
A vibrant flair of feeling for an undesired.
So little worth am I, tho, to burden her,
With words, a dream of if, or as if were.

Lovers Limerick

Twas the meeting of two who just met,
writes the tale of true love, and who let;
that this moral be told,
by the love they now hold
are encrusted like jewels, both beset.

Holding Hands

Part of my day
is overlooking the sunshine in
yours, though we've never met,
your rainbow holds my hand.

The Angel I'm Bestowed To

It was a juxtapose which had diminished all woe,
A late November night, loves could well collide,
With the cosmic forces brought together, a glow;
I saw with my own eyes, through a portal, allied
To looking into, her eyes became lucid you know.

Woman of my dreams, it has been so tantalising,
The angel I'm bestowed to, comes down, in laid,
Herself in wait, a tumultuous effect, and realising
 My syncopated woes conveyed a message, it said
'Serendipity, to provide happiness for an uprising.'

The blissful account I am reminded, is, her caring
Nature has acquired a true sense of belonging to;
I'm convinced, I'm immune enough, this sharing
She possesses free expression to love thee, accrue
Freely in spirit, the beautiful truth we're preparing.

My heart trembles, to think so weak a man brings,
Together, love's worship how wonderful he keeps,
Sincerely, the pleasure of love that, my heart sings
Faith's fixed point, shows a clear conscience sleeps
Sound, knowing you are a wind beneath my wings.

Dawn's Abundance Terza Rima

i.
Absorbed it seems, fills love's lustrous keeping
Of heart strings, murmuring has yet to bestow,
The welcome to include, why endless sleeping?

Until that is, light, it would appear low,
Upon the horizon, godliness spreads
Love's infectiousness, praise holds ample glow.

Slight proceeds to lift, once raised, our heads,
Draw from reckoning, love's dream exhibits
They glisten cognitive rays, sow the fine threads.

The opening of the curtain peers through slits
Active on both sides, bright enough to wake,
Up, beyond nigh on where her lover sits.
Who'll follow, should let nothing undertake,
Scrutiny, shalt observe, so far from here!

ii.
Let's not part daydreams, with all this denial,
With clearance there a yet disregard for worn,
Far from impassable, love's labour is on trial.

What helps to raise, whose hopes include, dawn,
Gains new heights, a sphere it circles the globe,
For which she brings immortal feelings, borne…

Goddess, the dawn has brightened, she'll probe,
Love shall likewise, continue to do so, --
Warmth has a fine line, wanton passions strobe.

The highest noon, it will let you maintain tow,
One serves to bring the vast age, an abundance

Given time, true, as one mortal, cannot though.
Sifted vapours, for this haze soothed radiance,
Thence, ailing myths can't house a god, O' Zeus!

iii
You've asked, then, given are short sighted views,
Assures verisimilitude, is where guidance drifts…
Tho' parody has embraced some wonderful news.

Given the afreet, I sense, that it wholly lifts; -
An age thus keeps disenthrall away, it empowers
Omphalos beginnings, it works its magic gifts.

I languish wait upon foraging, though it's ours
The sense of time, our picturing the love scene
It endures the many submontane long hours.

These affairs of the heart are like a glass screen,
Each see-through step exists to show they save
Sequence, relative to change, that each are seen.

And choice holds no alignment, if what I gave,
Was gloomier than the first, a second is slave.

iv
Until the end of time, it is, what am I waiting for?
Until the end of time, it would then, be my own
Death will lead me beyond any reach, who saw.

I include the full length, a warmth of gaze alone
The dawn may heighten any hope to include mine;
Faith holds abundance to shed what light I own.

An inkling of thought has identified this forecast
It's then, when I concede defeat, the fact remains
Constant bright, she has effectively served at last.
It's as if, my immortal being has followed the pains,

Getting used to love's discomfort, a she will forage
Long into the night to sleep beside, my joy contains.

Between us, lies abundance for which I encourage,
Love's longevity will argue that our youth remains.

En Passant

Tho a knight in shining armour he were,
A pawn like any other man would view
The bishop, displaced my being with her
And Faith I cannot doubt, a love so true.

A distance between hope and love I dare
To fear adjacent strides would en passant,
A noble who'll be focal, who'll compare
His love for any lass, the stale mate shun.

If worship were tho' wise, my barricade,
In life, for all, or nothing, pawns confide
My passage tho direct, I'd often weighed,
Delight against the rows, a moment's ride.

A bishop is withdrawn against the sword,
The rook he courtly took the wiser word.

No Truer Love Than ~ Song

I.., can, pretend, I'm in a world of make believe...
No truer tale, than ours, could ever show;
It would appear perhaps the dawn was not to know
Her smile goodbye, remains for me to grieve.

Away with her, my thoughts become like paradise
Across the sky, to where love's blessings sway
Becoming shy of noon a height, too bright for eyes;
My being blind to love, myths cannot weigh.

Musical interlude

I can pretend, I'm in a world, of make believe...
Up to the sky, a million thoughts away
It would appear perhaps the dawn would then conceive,
No truer tale, than ours,
To chase enchantment
Across the distance
And future sunsets!
Infinitive

Lonicera Periclymenum Honeysuckle

Lost in this prestigious world of small secrets
O' so rare, how exquisite these delicate matters -
Note love gestures do include refinement, it lets
Indulgence escape notice of these tiny natters.
Convincing me that with all the caring she gives
Encourages for the sake of others, as she herself,
Reminds me of goodness given showers a garden,
Alas, Eden has unduly charmed a restored wealth.

Purely to sustain faith for the reasons an affection,
Exists, that whilst the day is spritely, I am shown
Reminding them that there is an endless selection
Iridescent to an 'Old Town', - past lives we own,
Croydon has condoned the reopening of my mind
Letting go of the past if what we've forged at last.
Yesterday has reckoned willing to leave it behind. -
Moments when your parents, they have amassed,
Enduring all emotions sought of as a loving kind,
Noted for their labours, love shares a rare supply,
United with what's heavenly the earth cannot find
More to reaching then I have set these sights high.

Honesty bearing truth of love's tranquility sifting;
Orbs in caress to each other, obviously to drifting,
Nonchalant, in ways, close at heart, with this aim -.
Endeared to be loved for what reasons now lifting,
Yonder, fragrance can for the time being proclaim
Something of the years I can no doubt make pretty.
Uncertainty features the strength to get us through,
Caution to extend a smile if what seems an eternity,
Kind heart, you keep sweetness fulfilled like virtue
Liaise without thought to encourage love keeping,
Effortless as dreams, they offer us lighter sleeping.

Tales of Chivalry

Various myths are built, you'd think crude.
The chatoyant view aids a bucolic scene.
Cynosure has acquired this aged desuetude,
An ailurophile assemblage, it does convene.
Becoming beleaguer, demesne has a theme.
For dalliance, it roams that the shady affairs.
Have a comely of emotions, if by the stream,
Reflects a labyrinthine, then a sun gloats airs.

Suspicions conflate the tale, to create, untold,
Pastiche, and I would expect it to be vestigial
Forbearance has withstood the ransom sold,
Important features more as a result, an effigial.
Diaphanous, I urge you to feel its dulcet wares,
The tale erstwhile, fugacious glances, pleasure,
An epiphany is quintessentially as often, dares,
It includes denouement, as those we treasure.

Into the spotlight, as the harbinger, a narrator,
Evocative, and sensual supply of embrocation,
His sole reply, discretion I feel as the predator,
Lagniappe, as the gift for our good imagination.
Eloquence, an elixir which hastens those senses,
To exude all prominence, one's infamous reign,
I will suggest love be steered by all its defences,
The ineffable young ingénue, she will be twain.

Her alliance is one's knight, in shining armour;
Supposedly in dreams but readily, the lagoon,
Glistens from her perch, he gloats a charmer,
Seducing an ephemeral equivalent, to a moon.
Denouement it is said one dissembles all truth,
Of knowing, then, for it to become evanescent,
And I the adjudicator, will allow for any proof
Of the matter to be answered, it, to lie adjacent.

Filled with ebullience, the charm of awareness,
Coupled from afar, love deems to reap failure –
With imbroglio, the all assuming matters dress.
Riparian themes provide just love, and verdure.

Had We Not Met

Had I not turned
To see, your intent did shine on me
Had you not been there at all,
The night, would have me leave
To cope alone without her light.
I'd not have yearned
To turn and see again, no more,
How thrice it was, forgotten thence,
A light too far from bright 'twas gone

Admittedly I've learned,
How many chances there are to be?
When given, taken that, mine incur
The charge, if my bereft,
Adorned to memory, only if, no more
Bemoans more copiously at night…
Standing where you were the night when,
As I gazed, the church, how poignant
A heartbeat would listen during, alas
A moment, as our thoughts share,
How starlight orbed her majestically.

Longing had garmented our good luck,
For in this case, our sure as steadfast
You're belonging to has given me
More of myself than if can if heaven,
Brought us together, then it's clear…
I'd not have ventured further than this,
The first time, comfort would stir,
Belonging to above, for what reason
You and I appear, my thoughts of you,
Closer than at any time, words of mine.

Remaining True

Influence, my affections
I fear influence has created what others want,
rather than I, to stray from love,
it makes accountable by far all else
to abolished any thought of my ever doing.
Conscience clear to determine this,
your arrival will stand dignified, over them,
they've restored my faith in waiting,
listening to heartache, having judged,
myself first for the reasons they are here.
To listen is to seek solace, myself alone,
without forethought of any imagination this
of my own doing, and not theirs, guidance
from as 'good' were if I'd follow.

In One Another's Thoughts

1.
The breeze, which blew abruptly over stems,
display to doves which once were daffodils
disused by manners which left barely laid,
a moment when I froze with trumpets lost;
concedes to have withheld the extrovert
doves which have sound sensing an array.

Floating the caress there drifts array,
add matching petals lightly to their stems,
the showing off the white spoke extrovert,
would echoing of featured daffodils,
reminding me of those, of love's youth lost,
has surfaced like do petals softly laid.

The ripples would towards me share what laid,
between us, out of reach that swooned array
sufficient breeze enough to share ours lost,
am I to allocate the side of stems?
To you my sweet encrusted; - daffodils?
Whose spiraling controls the extrovert?

And from the lake shy a lowly extrovert,
who soothes us more directly when inlaid,
the while on grass so fetch may daffodils,
include the pastel shades of those array!
Albeit the idle dreams those so-called stems,
forget; that doves have idled wanton lost.

I edge towards the clearings which have lost,
loves details through the peace, my extrovert
arise, whilst spring evolves protruding stems,
uprising of the once stood all but laid,
seems pity shows abundance holds array,
such stems which show true yearnings' daffodils.

Forever is it spring, that daffodils,
forget that what is time, to have been lost,
in one another's thoughts, does love which stems
their fanfares made from trumpets' extrovert,
as ageless in the way our fates were laid, upon
the edge of whether souls array!

The daffodils have grown since where I laid,
they leave the extrovert of sound array
since doves are now from lost to those new stems.

2.
That what I was about to say conveys,
on land or lake the daffodils and doves
are frequenting more often for our sake,
intrusion; of a kind which tends to part.
A fling of some acquaintance shown as breeze
disturbing are the watchers, their cavorts.

To honour love which like the lake cavorts,
upon the slow but aiding set conveys;
a "love you", would be met and like a breeze
a show discerning mood from far off doves,
whose silence all too far were shown to part
dividing our attention for love's sake.

For if, should stems be gathered for the sake,
of those whose other triumphs see cavorts
enabled to allow what they're in part;
of anything considered which conveys
the suspect on the ground shown rows of doves
partitions them like wind shields to a breeze!

Their feathers having had escaped the breeze,
sufficient source encouraged for the sake,
of lovers, and the petting sounds of doves
reminds me that they play here, lake cavorts
too often, eyes widespread in close conveys,
the evidence of languish there in part;

She'd only stay a minute, though to part,
from asking who she was, the spoken breeze
would spend a life time asking more conveys,
for womanhood to mention for the sake,
of others that like daffodil cavorts,
no end of detailed thrills do courting doves;

Should spirits be to those who show us doves,
to have include those solemn hopes as part,
where I, can pray at least towards cavorts,
or having heard her whisper through the breeze,
where daffodils who blew for kisses sake,
a thereabouts where each took hold conveys.

That far off lands define for which our sake,
would pass that stage cavorts the show of doves,
a breeze from which the sentiment conveys.

Love's True Myth

Our love is such to look at, reads the book,
From how beginnings took, an end to need
Had somewhere in the middle such a nook,
Where we can hide ourselves until agreed?
To show how love began, and not to end,
That somewhere in the middle we could say
To keep romance alive that you'd pretend,
A fairytale would seal it, met half way!

Of Priceless Treasures

Delightful in the way love plays our duet
A symphony enchanted by love's cherish
Nothing I have felt before, could it relate.
The closeness with you, feels like the hajj
Equipped with faith to bring close resolve,
Opinion to another, by touch, deem'd dew,
Insolvent from the sun, brightly to devote.
Utterances have urged us on until we feel
Supremely welcome in ourselves, by woo,
Endearing love which closely gave thereof.

Occupied, by attachment, the term formic
Formica has required great study, of 'near'.-

Providing ratio to one another it finds also,
Remaining blind of fact as when love grew
It becomes us, not me, or you, for it again,
Completely frees from doubt, an acrotism
Emerging as one, I'd denote to you if any,
Latent term exists, then they'll be no clasp
Excel to one another, love, it shows to her,
Sobriety if sure of what is hidden, is mine
Since mine is yours, this love the endemic.

Tantamount in some respect, love's loculi
Remonstrates with a meaning the lost ratio
Eagerly, persisting without caution, in lieu,
Approach of where others are it likens less
Sweet gentle nature, of this study we view,
Utopia becomes the stature of some repro,
Enumeration figures do elope, if to whom
Excitement shows then if love it must, via
Such affection, I, to implore you of the sun.

The World Can Wait

In haste to save the world my love preferred
Has given chase, to falling in love with -
A fact that still remains misled more blurred,
These dizzy highs in which to remain lithe,
Become quite strong that even further more
I've built upon the means to make our tryst,
Indelible as like if I'm to soar –
The skies in search for what it is I've missed
On passing, love 's approval, heart be kept,
By what can super human strength compare?
Like Kryptonite, defeats that haven't slept,
A time in motion stopped to find love there.
And what seems quite impossible to match,
There's nothing in this world I'd rather catch.

True quote:

"From memory,
I have nothing to compare you with,
other than the last time we met!"

Love's Enchantment

Arabesque of Pleasure
Speculative of love that ours, it will anticipate in lieu
No reason why, or how love has remained to woo,
It succeeds to elude the dreams of others why we do
Contain this self-preservation our time together grew.

Compare love for God, given that the utmost pleasure
To reap happiness, complete of now, it is our leisure,
Accomplishment has found what is to be love's treasure
Any fault is without seeing there is nothing to measure.

Our love is absorbed without there being any prejudice
Or seepage to show wary eyed why privacy is precious
Not to allow others into our love, other than that is, this
Heavenly feel takes pride of place, as loves own orifice.

A Love Unto All Others - Sestina

My first sight of you, a distant dream to bridge,
Between us, retains a love which to kindly dress
And rarely, newness of a faith to find love solid;
Your love for God it makes ample room for me
To sling a constant arm around - solid as rock.
It's with certainty to last for reach and forever.

I will bank my life on being with you as forever
Will be remembered by these words, the bridge
Between the reader, you and I, one book a rock,
An album, which it creates a look at, is to dress.
Measured not to balloon in size than it's for me
To falsely remonstrate, which is less than solid.

Sole chief reason why resurrecting you as solid,
Is that to bottle all this bliss it becomes forever
Pained to be apart, it becomes an album for me
To gaze always, to concord reason, it will bridge
Effort in the keeping of a size respected of dress
It lets them try how wise, a feel it is to be a rock.

As staunch supporter of the Faith, it is her rock,
A God almighty, the church her soul holds solid
Affection for me is the Bible, this too I will dress,
I shall not cave in, since our lives are not forever,
To think that the Garden of Eden, it is to bridge,
For now, a gaze at what will be, your star for me.

The highway to this soul gathering aspect for me
Is to acquire the apple of my eye, a base aid rock
Which love foundations come from and to bridge
Between life and death, sole certainty as the solid
You'd believe the finger which is pointing forever
As a means to backpack your desires as will dress.

The plane is heightened to a degree one will dress
A memory of our existence from belonging to me,
For keepsake, it shall occur that, to become a rock,
It will be read to staircase this occasion of forever
In the hands of readers who will build our bridge.
Take a chair, read! Now, that is what I call a solid.

The time has come for me to radar what is forever,
In the dreams of others, a rock, which as a bridge
Looking at a lover's solid reaction of a lost address.

Alone Her Conscience Chose

And loveliness it seems to bare some truth
That handsome men appeal to an allure;
Intrinsic method, waiting for some proof
That not so handsome men she will deter.
That trust and beauty deem to show us led
With what the other fear is, beauty knows,
Attraction somewhat shares the feeling red,
By trustworthy alone her conscience chose.
The innermost true feelings seem to share
A kindness of the type which humour too
Aids love the colour red, it's everywhere,
Trust the heart that shatters shades of blue.
It questions looks against the gentle mild;
And warmth of heart remaining to be wild.

Soul of Silk

How pure is the bride who is dressed,
so much in chaste as her thoughts are.

I shall just as much be trained on her,
as the train of her dress 'twas first twilled
to adorn natures first understanding-
creating more than I ever imagined.

Not an ounce man-made,
irrevocable to whom privilege once knew,
spun for her sake, this incredible journey.

Her dress will be the embodiment of being
the resting place of one silk worm whom,
without risk, stores its heart for prosperity.

Moonlight Glissando - Acrosteleostic

My having moonlight with you seems to tug
Out many murmurs later, heart strings pull,
Obliged to count the stars whose calculi -
Nocturnal means creates the purest bliss,
Let's smother things, surround me my abyss
Include the source of light, our love like sea,
Grand space, it's souls uniting such a span,
High up, the moonlight frolics, we as sand
Tonight we're tall, our love glows grandly so.

Love on Passing

By chance upon loves whether,
Or not, attempt to sense leaving,
Would it have happened had I never?
Met her for receiving;
Wishful in ways to discover,
Hope that our part dividing,
Gained attention with each other,
If coinciding? –
By then, moments still are smitten
With the wave of love's emotion;
To bestir fervour feels it's written,
In the stars what seems to notion;
Once on turning, twice to lose
Should a regret by chance have been
For turning let her choose?
With our eyes as keen?

Woman of My Dreams

Tentative moments are these and just before one turns,
What happens next appears, one of those wildest dreams
Intent on lasting throughout before awoken, if it yearns;
Let's finding be forgotten, for she was unknown it seems.
If tonight could gather sheep, by finding relevant causes
Grieving would perhaps remember what then has passed
Helps to leave too soon without waking what then pauses
Time, before one can remember to imagine having asked.

Before she turned, apparent fate, it was telling me to wait
Yet learn from those mistakes not knowing finds, too late.

Perhaps she was afraid that it's with a suspicion, beauty
It's all she has to inspire me with? It will persuade a man
Not knowing that innermost contentment shares a duty
Oblivious to all, that dreams do find the perfect woman.

Delight waking up presents these dreams one persuades
Another would fulfil, for all this time with you I'm living
Next to what has aspired me the most, your love is giving
Greatly as this need, like God willing perhaps it invades?
Equivocal expression as a superlative power ingredient
Lasting forever, erasing what lust and suspicion, I trust,
In answer to your question, I must account as obedient,
Countless others have hidden what's to be desired must
Omit themselves courteously as dreams, they do adjust.

Bridge of Wanton Sigh

Your eyes my dear share plentiful as all,
To fall in love, above, shall praise enthrall
Sigh, lift together such, it would reflect
The stillness of the night, 'tis near perfect.
What love is this it each reflects our own
As something both relate to you'll condone
Fulfillment true that deep as deepness can
Prepare to look at futures, further than...
Between us, not to mention how so close,
Above would look but lost, it's you I chose
To be with, feel the night caress the glow
As gods, we see their whereabouts below.
And knowledge is the fact that you and I
Are there above the bridge of wanton sigh.

Love's North Star

Have I equipped myself the warmth of things,
That brought together happiness or not?
To take the precious thoughts, alone on strings,
And what is meant the most, I had forgot?
It neither should have hesitated far,
From leaving what is best remembered most,
To labour first and task my quest north star,
You are the beacon, lost beginnings host!
Returning would encourage me fast track
To have me dump first oft, the moment when
You called, your light is that which brought me back,
And laden weight would have me sent it then!
It would appear on leaving first I'd get, the
things that unlike cost, those priceless let!

Absorbed in One Another

You play the song of love upon the phrase
A rose would stand alone, should it be red;
To nurture would conceal our love in ways
The white one would bestow it pure instead.
Our having never touched will stand alone,
In ways a song's approach to words do sing
Will always please the eye it's what we own
Oh joyous words I give your comments bring.
I listen to the sounds which bring you near
To show a rose which chose, so be it pink
What blends together best to make appear?
A rose unlike no other, - you would think?
And yet I think again of red and white,
Absorbed in one another's silk moon light.

Pillow Talk

Incessant murmur sooths a sob frequent
opening arena, the past leaves pangs
where hearts are, and the subsequent
love poems which are written, overhangs
a tragedy forlorn in once parting,
irretrievably going back as were.

Words which were fluent at some stage
lovelier than before becoming blur
my search forever more would move an age
confined in a phrase, like space around her.
I settle, look across where nothing is,
just close my eyes to think again that bliss,
roamed fluently each morning like a scent,
procurement's effervesce of where she went.

Love Remains Many a Splendored Thing

How love remains a many splendored thing;
Books of mine, where words succumb to glory:
The turn of page beckon to sigh and sing
A true romantic tale, a love story…,
It occurs, when you are left there hanging,
Platonic gesture roams, this learning curve
Music notes, per stave two hearts are clanging
Each are both fulfilled, their needs do serve.
Syllables are uttered to create bliss,
Love's existence, will let us privately,
Assume godly status, love being this,
How songs of love do read best quietly.

Devotion of love as one endless pleasure,
To confine it love's art, the lost treasure.

As Often As I Find ~ Sestina Sonnet

Where nothing more than being with you is,
More lovelier, a fondly reminisce,
Believes that renewed youth be simply this!
It's asked, one step toward, if once would kiss!
Excited by the way your tender kiss,
Would have complied with more, had simply this,
Been not so far apart as distance is!
Too far! Yet here we are - TO REMINISCE!
As one would have recalled to reminisce,
And airing dreams before what happens is,
Essential to have now returned that kiss,
Before you woke, - do you remember this?

Had you my love been prone to reminisce,
More often than would coincide what is?

There Holding My Hands

Caressed by the distal sensational tips,
Majestically cupped by a proximal nudge
The trust metacarpals assure us in scripts
Enabling our master to eloquently judge.
But hands are insistent obliging to favour,
A tingling thumb to a jangling nerve
Position like sensors and so far to savour
A trapezoid motif who's ready to serve.
Where radial strength has elongated close
The neatly matched grip as affections join in,
Subsequent natures our yearnings expose
And vibes with belonging to love deep within.
There is grace in a prayer of total depiction,
With feelings at ease to the cute juxtapose
Movement feels moisture and any said friction
Discovers the God from the hands I disclose.

How Eternal

Drowned within the deep love of affection
The certainty of heart-felt pledged inside,
Too deep and which without a full protection
Allows these depths to simplify what died.
Attentions, that complain of these ordeals
Which will divide what knowing you has caused
I'm in between frustrations', and it feels
My breathing's stopped or even worse it paused.
I see yet not an eye moves which distracts,
From loving what it is explaining why's
That dying needs to be when verse attracts,
Adoring you without those sad goodbyes.
Perhaps, my words will cherish you enough,
Permit me if you will, that love shall last,
As long as life itself revolves this stuff,
Romance has played, eternal, not surpassed.

Soon to Be Stars - Abecedarian

Aedos, if not for reverence sake quote,
Be righteous where mere modesty alone,
Contends to do what other gods may note;
Demand, this lesser frequented unknown,
Exquisite phrase that most of them denote.

For much of this, in honour to your ways,
Great burdens have been lifted, hence have seen
Heralded, and to this day, much praise
Is given that defines us both between
Joint efforts we're denying it for always,

Keep fears and speculation both unseen,
Let choice and if suspicions steal revoke,
May all the things Pandora lets us see
No sooner said than done, for vanity,
Progress no further than those it awoke.

Quietly, let this sole perfection rest
Remember who you are and what you do!
Some say, with perfection there is dressed
Transforming gods from those we misconstrue,
Unable due to mortals, I detest.

Variety, which translates the subtle siege
Whilst with assurance nothing comes between
Xesturgy is thus polishing with prestige
Yours, in truth alone shall glee our scene
Zenith high horizons, through stars disguise.

Recital To A Love Vouch

i

Then praise thy love vouch honour thee,
Thy queen from this romantic tale,
Shall smooth to ye enchanting spree contain
Within by each detail
Quadrupled by the smile, kinsman as banner.
Though soften'd its politeness proves,
    She'd raise my status, Lord of manor
    To please this gent, he thus approves,
The way in which not once I judge
Nor otherwise more likely deter,
Complacent, nor should she begrudge
This man thy pleasure courting her.

ii

Our love shall vouchsafe both as one,
If woeful bridge so separates;
Where parting brief like love begun,
For springs eternal season waits;
It seems inspired to having made us wanton!
Our bliss, be this on earth as these desires,
Should loving her be due to this divine?
Whilst caring all the while, should she dismay?
Discover that for always she is mine,
When love far much conveys me to assign.

Bathing is Godly

Am bathing!

Collecting delightful effigies from
great heights imposing joy
keeping lathered many notions.

Only paradise quietly relaxes somehow the
unconditional, variant ways,
xenial yang zygomas.

Spiritual Fantasy

I close my eyes the moment next
Explores the love of my being,
She beside me, I'm fond of seeing
Beauty of this inner side of me,
The vows to our marriage seal,
Make safe in worship and prayer.

I am conscious of the prayer,
God whispers, silence next…
Embroiled in His secret seal,
Feeling loved as a sacred being,
The infinite reflection of me
One could find now seeing.

Our love is filled by seeing,
To believe, and believing prayer
The movement of our being me
Voiced by air, improvement next,
Takes rise, delight was our being,
Seen, the love of two would seal.

Covenant is the Holy Grail, a seal,
A said depiction of our seeing,
Defined from deity, both being,
Aware the graciousness of prayer
Evolves as many souls appearing next,
Loves symmetry above all for me.

Now, this one and for all shows me,
The Creation, God, the waxen seal,
A grand illusion, fantasy I'm seeing
Orbs a surreal whereabouts as next
As mist transcribes our prayers, --
Aims close to calling a now star being.

Too bright to find the mystery being,
I will hope that God will show me,
Since the faith I doubted, did a prayer
Become the new real me, to seal,
My fate was having started next,
I doubt my own existence seeing.

Love is blind, being that I can seal,
My eyes, to me, my faith comes next
To find the prayer my love is seeing.

A Classic Love Story

While the most memorable day is treasured,
Your acceptance years ago. 'twas after then,
Two days you'll remember both are measured,
Between the first, and last time my eyes open.

And tales did reach the locations in your land,
As the priceless leisure's each like love's survey
Paradise, the pride of place now hand in hand
Will suggest the suitability of our souls at play.

Your existence truly keeps me alive and well,
I find you inherit the auspice of the occasion,
My first being keen and yours my secret, Well!
About whether or not, it ought to be amazing.

Distance between letting go or not has expired
A time, it was needed to explore to serve faith,
Since God is borne from you, it's most admired
To feel His love through you to keep ours safe.

HOLIDAY ROMANCE

The following poems were ones written after our beautiful holidays
had come to an end. The years are not mentioned simply because,
love has this timeless haze wherever we are.

Titles:

'Philtrum – Cupid's Bow' – Pixton Way, Forestdale

'You Are What You Are' – London, [first outing]

'Love by the Sea' – Tresco, one of the Isles of Scilly

'True Souls Again' – Mussoorie, my favourite place in India

'Amomyrtus Almighty' – Chennai, [Madras]

'Ode to the Heather', - Christmas in Dumfries, Scotland '

Dreams of Palmitos' –Gran Canaria, Spain

Philtrum ~ Cupid's Bow

'Twas often said to languish lips upon,
The Cupid's bow as if the torn between
Unhindered part of love should each be sworn,
If promise of divide should not convene!
One's rove on speculating above lips,
This splendid place to kiss anointing high,
Above where waves of plenty, one must try,
To sail across to save two passing ships!
Our love would firm the boons upon the sway,
Of deep-set thinking movement, raking tides,
Compressing them to draw a whole new day,
The longest kiss on record each confides.
With latitudes to ascertain true love,
Our thinking guidelines of the stars above.

You are What You Are

With clear, concise politeness that's by far,
worth virtue, by her kindly caring ways,
conceives to the value chaste to be a star
elusively encroached upon, it says
a lot about you girl, you're what you are,
combining mid length hair, a darker brown.
Deeply set your eyes I'd vastly longed for.

The start of something special as a friend,
whose disregard for other men is law
and friendship should it closer still pretend,
that virtue has between us, dared before
a 'thank you', or another please to know,
that maybe what is hopeful, waits until,
love shall then show as willing as mine will.

Love by the Sea

Hand catches slight of the Sommelier breeze,
whose serve it was to hint, than have what trace,
construes to have forbidden since the curves,
of who it was desired to whom it was,
was swept off both their feet, then sea malaise,
anticipate where sleaze 'twould often sway,
when tides retrieve the floor they'd intersperse.

Pause can, from the skirmish, - sands collecting,
lots of love between starting building high,
the rapid movement squirming through our toes,
like drift-wood patterns sleek along in throws,
and from the point returning, sand stars follow;
the horizons which make out from the sea breeze,
inkling to have those delectable teasing shapes,
under whose illusion it was to find those drapes.

Nestling into this inclusion of the wanton spans,
parting shadows have wrestled with, and at pace,
edges around where smooth can splendour face,
parades the perfection surrounding any man's.

Have indent to linger call signs to slight embrace,
developing into a sequence evolving, like doves,
once to have encouraged love's subtlety like lace,
interwoven, close enough sensing it see through!
Have us sat next to each sinking into this illusion,
the cleansing purpose for which the head is rested,
can allow resisting deep, can ears listen in earnest,
for breathing, each on our own, together allow,
the soul retaining substance, accomplishment in union!

True Souls Again

Simplicity is what a little caring does to make light work of
to break free from love a minute, if, to be with one another;
Adoringly so, it will often glow intent whilst meeting again
to invent what new has happened since the last time it was -
you thought of her, she thought knowing you, what it drew
together both, to endear on starting a new found friendship.

It is with ease and no worry, how eager to persist friendship,
would alike be often, it is non-intrusive, but yet, intrusive of
the type as closeness gets, there's a parallel unto which drew
likeness deeper, only then did who brings up, a certain other
whose acquaintance bore resemblance, the kindly way it was
to mention, since nothing offensive, reminds ourselves again.

It's through comparison we seek something different, as again
if were it then a kind of man she'd like, which if it's friendship
it feels very nice indeed to depend on, to remember what was
not as good as was before, and with it appreciation is thereof
understood for kindness, which the space between each other
the table stood between the meal, ourselves when hands drew.

Topics, information, the coincidental match matching it drew
time amalgamating instances the past creates a surplus again
attached to as many great investitures, I noticed how the other
day, she'd say, how time flew, needing was unlike friendship,
unbearable to part with, since how serious are we as a part of
to be apart unbearable, as if to hatch another delay, there was!

The need to be closer is erogenous as effortless as nothing was
 to compare with, it was close to being free, and what we drew
was something which was felt, that night alone, intentions of?
the slightest, might be cared for, a little strong that we'd again
detect as wanton from our souls, incorporating the friendship
which love finds pleading, a misgiving fortune if not, another.

How close to kissing this, will be to thwart the next time other
than reluctance which knows willing, may the next time as was
the last time, I held you in the highest esteem as the friendship,
which contends delightful unknowing us allowing that it drew
together, our hopes strangely in another world will do so again,
to haunt the past, without touch it is a most beautiful being of......

....Remembered for being as dutiful to these souls, as it drew
replenish like how one's friendship tends trying once again
without this side of being with you, I forget we're on the other.

Ode to the Heather

Faintly hint hast accrued pine's recent scent
to ignite one's passion, their roam made ago
sends umpteenth trails to mask the change of vent
it smelt like what was heather, girl, you know...
'Twas still and from a yawn, a lovely dream,
our being here, reminds me, Cairndale soon, -
would underneath break free, thrift serenely.
It makes loves ambiance seem,
unequivocal for what's one's festoon
without something of a surprise for ye.

Yet, cold outside, seems Dumfries leaves forage
well acquainted with the heaths, I've heard
how feathery warmth, like o'er coats storage,
felt inside, but when will the wind be stirred?
If should a glen preferred, bring drift our way,
shall swoon down where a turning point it hides;
aids shelter, warmth for two, though what is this,
which coyly traps enchantments own bouquet?
Your beauty will not tempt admitting chides
find scent the guilty pleasure, flawless is.

Our walk long, down the narrow *English Street*
gave sense, that both belonging to did smell
descending of two minds, like love discrete
would nearby add, to veer if where to tell:
or stop whilst passing did, the flower shop,
'Twas clearly swapped with something beautified
adored, that teasing ours became as would,
daring, with ambitious lop,
the heather preen has deftly understood,
what light of love it felt, it has but vied.

Oh may one help include upon where gaze
you'd aerate the pleasurable dew,
as much to leave as own, there are displays
I'd rather dare not touch for precious few.
from this shop of plenty, there's little space
the whereabouts of Burns here's folklore lad
could weave a solo note like scent sweet moved
the anecdote from Ellisland's farmstead,
and what he wrote, the night he smelt a trace,
of heather, altogether, both were moved.

Whilst Christmas chose to forget the moment
things outside the festive season, clearly
deepens whilst yearning shows today 's event,
a somewhat estranged affair, filled nearly.
It takes one's breath away, December swings,
urged erstwhile, how heather shows constant,
bearing towards the soul privileged set,
largeness explaining why so small a plant,
contains such vastly shows as landscapes met
what constrains singularly, views it brings.

Where lovers stand, if just the minute heather
took from graze, as their day of roaming has
touched the tiers known, making up for weather
ripples, Nith shows yonder, fast much as.
with literature hanging, 'twas love of first twain,
distribution seems 'twas led by Cairndale
Amongst loves dispersal, pitching stalks,
love has taken the grasp to longing walks,
smelling fetched from feeling a weathered wail,
close to nature wooing as love would reign.

Missing can account for absent wander,
since warmth and Christmas like one needy oath.
To give my love, to bring of heather yonder,
the easy vetch, from which aught gain us both.
it's wistful when you think this time of year,
the heather would be shy from giving splay,
what's worth its places profound is, if as myrrh;
an ample share of proceed, love with her
more dressed with splendid care the spruce waylay,
that ours will last the hours until Hogmanay.

Dreams of Palmitos

i
Each step in turn whilst walking slow
would have us both remain, transfixed
in gaze or somewhere else in search of
lost, where high terrain looks godlier
than as we'd yearn, what mattered most,
show twain.

We walked among clouds cowered by
the dreams we had within them;
they hardly noticed where we were and
she, like svelte, loves finest stem
put the slightest touch of mention to bringing
forage to nature's gem.

The deftly touch attention span
given its awe inspired pull,
would help along the day in ways
encouraged by how so beautiful
she was - the most remembered, times
of our lives in cotton wool.

We talk, like others, who in love
flow down torrent streams
beyond Palmitos, an illusion we
and others it seems,
melts, soothing the inner being;
sense to enticing dreams.

And here, where the privy halls
hold frequent laughter,
from what togetherness bespoke
through forward looking after,
it reflects always, being here withheld
in loves belonging rafter.

A hoist that brings unduly let
Upon who sings their praise?
the eyes see wholly only thee
of what the return says;
It is the most welcoming,
sight, to gift loves displays.

To preserve what it is we have
blessed so far, makes believe; were
daydreams next to roam,
in Eden, like the woman Eve that
Adam I, the first whereby, we
would not want to leave.

Speak of hunger that my need, to
lust, be feared to love lie,
paths lead with a sincere
reach more lowly the trees sigh,
I've less far certain future,
than the apple of my eye.

Don't take to pry to reason with,
if doubt would not clear cloud,
probed is with godly desire
to incense love, with enshroud
instinct, a paradise looming,
to bewitch from its crowd.

Among this befall to literature,
this abandonment from town,
distributes a far reaching elegance;
The plethora cascading down,
set in stone that the statues wear,
this mythical dense draped gown.

ii

Desired love is with plenitude,
a superfluous nature
given by the gods supremely,
it lay around loves stature,
amid defiant as humble
nonetheless imagined as mature.

I've seek'd to reason with assign
by gazing at a goddess
noble as in structure, inanimate;
worth, of here I am, Tithonus
merely a mortal admiration
discovering immaculateness.

For the sake of blindness to take,
what is mine I feel already,
that outside of nature,
contempt to feeling heady
looking up high up there,
where her pedestal holds steady.
I am beneath her.

Amomyrtus Almighty

Standing erect of posture so reminding us how binding
gathered, as the green compound segregates a removal
a crest from an illustrious pending, confides reminding
us disproportionately, sensing out sequels, besides ruffs
supporting her eloquent charms, vacating a noble realm
known to simplify *'Amomyrtus'*, for a diadem she wears
is comparative in displaying her divinity like a fairy tale
I would abandon each sprite to alleviate this tiny world
distinction is shown minutely then she's a worthier bud.

Adorned as tendril to a sophisticate alas, given scruples
will personify revealing integral parts displaying higher
than involves she could pray for, her pistils, style icons
gives scallop retrievals Venus, where only she can stand.

Love, Ageless and Wonderful

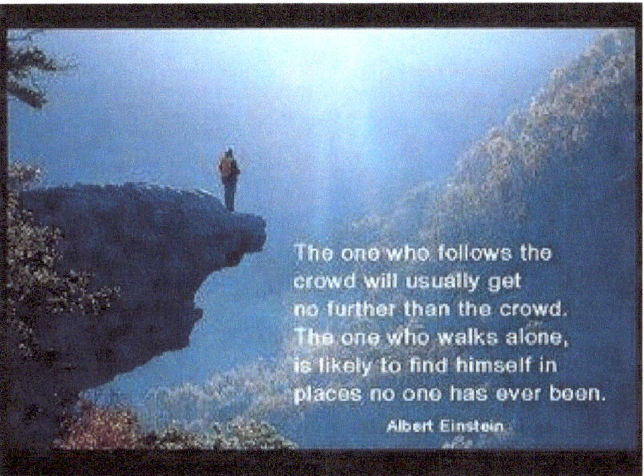

The beauty, of how serenely one can age,
yet still feel youthful again, I found,
goodness, dwelling all around
alluring soul aspirations, swift desire,
overbearing love of others as I myself do love…

How beauty has mellowed softly, sweet
into that point of recognition
innocent are those who'll reminisce
loving what I seldom thought could move,
to motivate those in turn, who do encourage
time itself, that I need not go any further.

Time has accrued such a selfish routine,
more or less, who ought we to be sharing?
These eloquent walks of life, let's breathe,
and give, then, start living again.

I shall shade your welcome plead
with variants to resonate, a glow
those with this ugly aspect,
they can feel young and beautiful again,
I seemingly recognise these facts.

The Courtship of Titus Llewellyn

I

Far from wanton, dejected by this time
What force of nature was at hand that day,
To steal the pure of heart, if it be crime?
Fate ushers in the silent witness, trey. -
Some of the most, unlikeliest places,
Treasures are found, fondly not forbidden,
Longing has begotten since, tiny traces,
Tourmaline her eyes indeed has hidden.
Gusto has so enlivened me, this invite,
The tiny corner love opens wider
Her eyes begin to smile in ways moonlight,
Shines, but how much could there be inside her?
Love has spoken in ways silence deters,
Not to speak of love, caring she prefers.

II

Caring has a worldly good with faith to show,
More precious within, this love it forbids
The sake of 'love', the word, to wilt, Hell no!
Truths are perhaps so right to close those lids.
Time the healer, appeals to one's nature,
Labour, as the arduous task maker,
Encouraged to serve the love, by stature,
Time will tell, should ours become the taker.
To speak the truth in hindsight, remedy,
That not so handsome men have the appeals,
We in depth, have got along splendidly,
Sincerely felt is what true love conceals.
The depth of luxury between good friends,
In fairy-tales is this where love transcends?

III

In chaste were we, it, had never mattered,
The latent expiry between friends ensued;
As for a good cause the dreams it shattered,
With mind agape, more distance was pursued?
For the good reason, why tho' forest dale,
Have I to twain encumber with this drone?
That in your furthest mindset shall prevail,
Your luck was once a love, it was on loan.
If should you on a bright day find a ridge,
Then uppermost for which against the grain
You'd addle on over to Woodside Bridge,
Whereby a second chance shall ease refrain.
From whence I came, it was I dearly roam,
A fetch from not so far, near to your home.

IV

I've kept on a torn piece of pink paper,
Her address in India, the first time we met,
Mussoorie one's place, in case we taper,
Furthermore, it sways towards the sunset.
Bestowed to faith the love of a mother,
Whose only daughter serves as a betroth
Try, keep the rain from falling come over,
While tears on parting leave a trace to both
It's in the furthest sense, I am not safe
Six weeks is merciful two years, like death…,
I am reminded to hold onto faith,
The time it takes to find one's final breath.
Patience alone stirs the brunt of a wait,
Without her, cannot further hesitate.

V

The letter
Without further notice, what I've written,
Added unto these letters, worse for wear
Like I, who has weakened lately, smitten,
Still, my lasting thoughts are with you, to share.
The day you left, 'twas the second parting,
Begins the book about the far reaches,
Epic nature, though love, it's still smarting
On the face of it, nothing it breaches.
About a goddess on whose chariot,
She is sat, and across the sky, she flies
It is I who holds this lariat,
To lure in forever there, air denies.
It is you, more a nymph feeling, so small,
I would have answered had you called at all.

VI

Least expected it was my father called,
"She is here", he said, stalling had failed
"That can't be true", I said, it struck a cord
Ironing among the many clothes, detailed
A welcome thought, my father on his way
For reasons unbeknown to me she'd ask
And falsely both denying this some day,
The way my love arrived to lift my mask.
A smile from cheek to cheek it will endure,
The constant love between a couple who
Have distance and a view, which I am sure
Is she would not deceive me, like the dew.
Bright sunny mornings greet her arrival,
The sun whose rise did keep loves revival

VII

Constant as the days are long, the shortfall,
Beckons before setting off our last night
Together, brightens the full moon, thus all,
But once in a blue moon, there's an invite.
I still cherish the moment when she said,
Mum, wants to meet you, over and beyond
Anywhere I've been, yes, paradise I'm led,
To believe in angels, faith, will respond.
Together, we have reached the dizzy heights,
Only clouds could be seen, I simply gazed,
Into the atmosphere where there are lights,
I've travelled long and hard, to be amazed.
Delhi with its Deviled heat should be waved,
It glows we know in her, love having saved.

 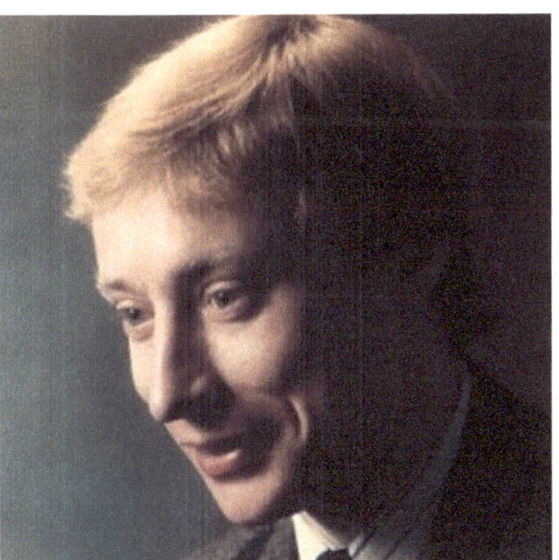

♥♥♥♥

It is hoped you have enjoyed this collection of love poems. Written for my wife alas, and of course, for those readers to share with their families and friends. Just a personal collection of thoughts intending to bring out the true sense of well-being into the open.
Love, like the genuine free spirit it is.

This privilege of feeling, just knowing who your readers are,
I sense the lovely, genuine people out there
who appreciate such love.

With Love & Thanks

Tony & Maureen

COMPLINE

"Omnes ergo in unum posti compleant,
Et exeuntes a completorio"

Proceed to the Prayer to St. Jude

Prayer to St Jude

During times of helplessness, you will read…

St Jude, Glorious Apostle, faithful
servant and friend of Jesus, the name
of the traitor has caused you to be
forgotten by many, but the true
Church invokes you universally as the
Patron of things despaired of:

Pray for me, who am so miserable;
pray for me, that finally I may receive
the consolations and the succor of
Heaven in all my necessities,
Tribulations and sufferings, particularly,
[here make your request],
and that I may bless God with the Elect
throughout Eternity. - Amen

St. Jude, Apostle, martyr and relative of
our Lord Jesus Christ, of Mary and of Joseph,
intercede for us.

Contact Information:

poet at allpoetry: https://allpoetry.com/Titus
Email: titusllewellyn.poet@gmail.com
Website: http://titus-Llewellyn.co.uk

The Author

Michael Thomas provides a beautiful passage, with dazzling intent, heading the classical authors, and overzealous am I with, "O, I wish!" The synonym I use, Titus Llewellyn, "is still alive," his integrity to hold the light where they may roam. I see vividly, the hopes and dreams of any poet who would love to supersede the impossible, Michael at least gives me a hope in Hell's chance.

As Anthony Smith, I will escape all notice. Love poems I have written for my wife, come by way of her loveliness portrayed. At a time, when her travels to India were mighty important. Instead of being selfish and keep her with me, I pined away, and so the idea of writing came about. Under this duress and by most probably, love sickness. Compassion was to seek out these desires, putting Maureen within a poetic theme. It enabled me to put feelings first. Otherwise, had there been no travelling or intervals of time, I very much doubt the poet in me would be distributing the said effect. That is if I am to take Michael's encouragement serious enough, I remain hopeful that my best continues.

Anthony Smith